The Rare Shell

FASTBACK® Horror

The Rare Shell

JANICE GREENE

GLOBE FEARON
Pearson Learning Group

FASTBACK® HORROR BOOKS

The Caller	The MD's Mistake
The Disappearing Man	Night Games
The Hearse	Night Ride
Live Bait	No Power on Earth
The Lonely One	**The Rare Shell**
The Masterpiece	Tomb of Horror

All photography © Pearson Education, Inc. (PEI) unless specifically noted.

Copyright © 2004 by Pearson Education, Inc., publishing as Globe Fearon®, an imprint of Pearson Learning Group, 299 Jefferson Road, Parsippany, NJ 07054. All rights reserved. No part of this book may be reproduced or transmitted in any form or by any means, electronic or mechanical, including photocopying, recording, or by any information storage and retrieval system, without permission in writing from the publisher. For information regarding permission(s), write to Rights and Permissions Department.

Globe Fearon® and Fastback® are registered trademarks of Globe Fearon, Inc.

ISBN 0-13-024518-6
Printed in the United States of America
1 2 3 4 5 6 7 8 9 10   07 06 05 04 03

1-800-321-3106
www.pearsonlearning.com

Nick was walking past the shop when he saw the seashell. He stopped and stared at it in the shop window. It looked like many shells Nick had seen before, except something about this one made it seem special. Years ago, as a boy living near the ocean, Nick had collected seashells. But he had long since gotten rid of all of them, giving some away and throwing the rest out.

Now he suddenly had the urge to buy this one. In fact he wanted it very much.

He pushed the shop door, which opened with a loud buzz.

Nick glanced around the shop at the fancy lamps and vases. It was an expensive-looking place—too expensive for him. It was also terribly hot and stuffy. Nick loosened his collar and walked up to the counter. A short, pink-faced man was standing there, his lips curved in an odd sort of smile. He leaned toward Nick. His voice was very soft. "You'd like to buy the shell," he said.

Nick nodded. The man went to the front window, came back, and put the shell on the counter. Nick picked it up carefully in his big hands and turned it over. He felt strange, dizzy. On a tiny label the price read: $105.

"It's so expensive!" Nick said. "Is it rare?"

The man laughed—a high, thin laugh that gave Nick the creeps. The man reached for the shell with small, stubby fingers. "Perhaps it will not be too expensive for someone else," he said.

"No, wait," Nick said, pulling the shell back. He didn't know why, but he knew he had to have it. He wrote out a check with a shaky hand. The hot air of the shop made it hard to breathe.

The pink-faced man examined the check and smiled slowly. "Well, Mr. Weston . . ." he said. He gave Nick a bag for the shell. Nick hurried out of the shop, his legs weak and his head spinning. The pink-faced man watched him leave, his lips curved in a strange grin. "Come back soon, my friend," he said. "Soon." His soft voice was almost a whisper.

Nick walked down the street, taking in great gulps of cold winter air. Why had he acted in such a crazy way, he wondered? What ever made him pay more than a hundred dollars for a seashell? What good was a seashell? He would return it tomorrow, he decided, and get his money back.

He crossed the street to a tall building. The sign on the front said, "Glenview Apartments." He went inside and walked up the narrow staircase to his own apartment on the second floor. The sign on his door said, "Manager." As he opened the door, a thin elderly man came down the hall.

"Hi, Nick!" said Lennie Faber.

"Hello, Lennie," said Nick.

"I'm still looking for my glasses," said Lennie. "I certainly hope I find them, so we can have our card game tonight."

"Yeah," Nick said. "Maybe I'll see you later." He stepped inside and sighed. Lennie was a lonely man since he retired. Their weekly card game really cheered him up. But Nick wished there weren't going to be any game tonight. He was getting tired of playing cards with Lennie. He just wanted to be alone.

He opened the bag and took his shell out. Now, away from the surroundings of the shop, it didn't look very special. And it certainly didn't look like it was worth $105.

He thought of all the shells he had collected when he was a boy. Then he held this new one up to his ear, just as he had done years ago, to see if he could hear the ocean.

First he heard the distant, roaring sound of the sea, that he remembered so well. And then he thought he heard a voice. . . . *Mr. Weston* . . . Nick shook his head and then listened again. . . . *Mr. Weston* . . . the sound came once more, like a distant voice, a voice under water. He felt dizzy and weak, as he had in the shop that afternoon. He listened once more. *Just open your window, Mr. Weston, and your little problem will be solved.*

Nick stared at the shell, his heart pounding. He tried to clear his head. *Nick, he told himself, you must be imagining things.* He put the shell down and decided to make himself dinner.

As he stood in the kitchen cooking some vegetables, Nick thought about the strange voice he heard coming from the shell. *That's great, Nick,* he said to himself. *First you start talking out loud to yourself every day. Now you're starting to hear voices that aren't there. It's starting to get to you.*

He knew what the problem was, too, although he didn't want to admit it. It was all the time he spent by himself. Aside from running into the other tenants in the hall, or having to fix something in their apartments, Nick had very little contact with people. He liked to keep to himself. He only played cards with Lennie once a week because the old man practically begged him to play.

Nick had been the manager at the Glenview Apartments for almost a month. He had just recently moved to the city from another state. So he didn't have any friends. But he didn't mind. He had always been something of a loner. He just never made friends easily.

Now, maybe, it was beginning to affect him. Being alone most of the time, not going out very much. Perhaps it was causing him to imagine things. Like voices coming from a seashell. He laughed and said to himself, *You're going soft in the head, Nick ol' boy.*

When dinner was ready, Nick sat down at the table. As he did so, his eyes caught something in a corner of the room, on a cabinet. It was Lennie's glasses! *How did they get there?* he wondered. Funny that he hadn't noticed them before today.

Suddenly Nick felt very dizzy. He heard the distant voice from the shell again: *Just open your window, Mr. Weston, . . .* Nick picked up the glasses, walked over to the window, and opened it. He held the glasses far out over the ledge and dropped them. The sounds from the street below helped to clear his head. The dizzy feeling slowly disappeared. He wasn't sure what had happened. He looked outside. On the sidewalk below were bits of metal and broken glass. He felt cold and weak all over. *I better go lay down on the couch*, he thought.

After a while Nick got up, picked up the shell, and stared at it. He told himself: *It's just a seashell making a weird noise. It didn't make me do anything.* But he felt a little scared—because he wanted to listen to the shell again. He quickly put it back in the bag, and then put the bag away on a high shelf. He decided to go to bed. Tomorrow he'd buy Lennie a new pair of glasses.

The next morning Nick woke up and groaned. The first thing he'd have to do today was deal with Mr.

Minter. Everett Minter, who lived on the first floor, drove him crazy sometimes. Minter complained about everything. He complained about the noise his neighbors made, the smell of the trash bin in the back of the building, and especially about the bad job he felt Nick was doing as the manager of Glenview Apartments. Today Nick had to fix Minter's kitchen faucet. Minter said it made a loud, thumping noise when the water was turned on.

Nick got his plumbing tools together and then made breakfast. He was sitting at the table, eating, when the sound of a violin began in the room above him. Nick groaned again. The Bennetts lived upstairs, and their 11-year-old daughter, Christy, played the violin. Christy was a nice kid. But sometimes she practiced the violin for hours, and Nick was sick of hearing it.

Nick picked up his toolbox. It was time to leave. Minter was expecting him. On the way out, he went right past the shelf with the shell on it. He tried to keep walking, but something made him stop. He wanted to listen to the shell again. He *needed* to listen to it again.

He held the shell up to his ear. The soft roaring began. Then the strange, underwater voice: *Mr. Weston* . . . Nick felt dizzy. He leaned against the wall. *Just hold your toolbox in your left hand, Mr. Weston, and your little problem will be solved.*

Nick shivered and put the shell back in the bag. Something about the voice scared him. But it hadn't made him throw Lennie's glasses out the window, he told himself. Nothing could make him do something he didn't want to do. He decided that he wouldn't listen to the shell again. This was the last time. He went out the door and down the stairs to Minter's apartment.

An hour later, Nick was walking up the narrow staircase, feeling pretty good. He had stopped the noise in Minter's faucet, and for once Minter had been satisfied with Nick's work. It hadn't been easy. Minter had hung over his shoulder the whole time, making suggestions. And his pesky cat kept jumping up on the counter and playing with Nick's tools.

"Hi, Mr. Weston." Christy Bennett was walking down the stairs, her violin in her hand.

"Hi, Christy. How's it going?" said Nick. He started to feel dizzy.

Christy was coming closer. She was two steps away from him.

"Pretty good," she said. "How about you?"

... *hold your toolbox in your left hand, Mr. Weston* ... Very quickly, Nick switched his toolbox to his left hand. Christy banged into it, losing her balance.

"Aaaaaaah!" she screamed. She flew

forward, bumping into Nick's shoulder and knocking him back against the railing. Then she rolled to the bottom of the stairs, landing on her stomach with a heavy THUMP—and a smashing sound.

For a moment she lay still. Nick froze. Then she moved. He ran down to her, his face white, his breath coming in gasps. He helped her get up. "Are you all right?" he asked.

"I'm really sorry, Mr. Weston. I'm always crashing into things. Are you okay?" she asked.

"Yes. Are *you* all right?" asked Nick.

"I'm okay," she said. They looked at the violin. The wood was broken into long splinters. The strings stuck out in all directions.

Christy gently scooped up the pieces of her smashed violin. She hurried past him, tears rolling down her face.

Nick almost ran to his room. He locked the door and sat down at the table, his head in his hands.

Just open the window, the voice in the shell had said. *Just hold your toolbox in your left hand*, was the second message. And he had broken an old man's glasses and knocked an 11-year-old kid down the stairs. Nick felt cold—cold and scared. This time he wasn't imagining things. The shell *was* sending him messages—and seemed to be controlling his actions.

But what scared him the most was the feeling that he wanted to listen to the shell again.

No, Nick told himself. He would take the shell back to the shop—now. He'd get his money back. He'd buy Lennie a new pair of glasses. Maybe he'd have enough for a violin, too. He put on his jacket, zipped it up, and walked to the door. He stopped, his hand on the doorknob. He shut his eyes tight. He couldn't leave. He wanted to listen to the voice in the shell. *Just this once*, he told himself. *Just one last time.*

Nick held the shell to his ear. The dizzy feeling came on very strong. Then he heard the distant, underwater voice: *A good, sharp knife, Mr. Weston. Just use a good, sharp knife, and your little problem will be solved.* Chills went up and down Nick's spine. A knife. He would stay away from knives. He'd stay away from everybody for a few days.

He turned on the TV set and sat down. He barely paid attention to the movie that was on the screen. He felt very tired. The phone rang.

It was Minter, and he was annoyed. "Nick, you're going to have to come down here and fix this faucet again. Now it's started dripping."

Nick's hand on the phone started to shake. He closed his eyes and saw Lennie's glasses smashed on the pavement, and Christy tumbling helplessly down the stairs.

"Well?" Minter said, sharply.

"Please, Mr. Minter," Nick said in a hoarse voice. "Couldn't it just wait a little while?"

"No, it can't. My wife and I are having guests for dinner tonight, and we certainly need our faucet working properly."

"I'll be right down," Nick said. He didn't know what else to say.

Nick hung up the phone and wiped his forehead. He was starting to sweat. His hands felt cold and clammy. *I don't want to go down there*, he thought. *I don't want to get near that guy, not the way I feel now.*

He thought of calling Minter right back and making up some excuse. But he knew that that wouldn't do any good. Minter would just get angry and say he was going to complain to the owner of the building.

He was always threatening to do that. Nick knew that the owner would be upset if a longtime tenant like Minter made a complaint about him. And Nick couldn't afford to lose this job.

He gathered up his tools and walked slowly downstairs to Minter's apartment. He would be careful, he told himself. He wouldn't get near Minter. And he wouldn't let Minter make him mad.

Minter stood on one side of the sink, his arms folded. "Look at that drip," he said. "Let's see if you can do a decent job this time."

Nick realized that Minter was going to stand right next to him, watching him work, as he had before.

"You don't have to stick around, Mr. Minter," Nick said nervously. "I'll tell you when I'm finished working."

"Nonsense," said Minter. "I'm going to stay right here and make sure you do it right."

Nick started to work, loosening the faucet handle. His hands were sweaty. The wrench slipped.

"Be careful!" Minter said. "I don't want you making a big, ugly scratch."

Nick tried again. Minter's cat jumped up on the counter and began batting at the dripping water with its paw.

"Don't be a pest, kitty," said Minter.

The cat paid no attention to him.

Nick got the spout loose. He began taking it apart, trying to keep his hands from shaking.

"Here, give those to me before you drop them," said Minter. He laid the parts out carefully on the counter. The cat reached over and began to bat them with its paw.

"Kitty, you're in the way," said Minter, picking up the cat.

It's about time you noticed, thought Nick angrily.

"I'm going to put her in the bedroom," said Minter. "Don't do anything until I get back." He went out of the room holding the squirming cat.

Nick stood up and stared at the parts lying on the counter. He had no idea why the faucet was still leaking. He was having trouble thinking at all.

Minter came back. "Figure it out yet?" he said.

Nick didn't answer.

Minter bent over the sink. "Well, it's clear to me you need a new washer. This one's shot."

Nick felt a flash of anger. *If it's so clear to you*, he thought, *why didn't you say so in the first place?*

Minter poked around Nick's toolbox. "Here, try this," he said, holding up a new washer.

Nick tried it. It was too big. Nick took a little file from his toolbox and began filing down the edges of the washer.

"You'll never get anywhere with that

thing," said Minter. "Hold on a minute."

Nick stopped filing and stood very still. He felt dizzy.

Minter opened a drawer and pulled out a knife six inches long. Its blade flashed in the light. The brightness hurt Nick's eyes.

"What you need is a good, sharp knife," said Minter. He handed the knife to Nick and bent over the sink.

A roaring sound filled Nick's head. A roaring sound and a message: *Just use a good, sharp knife* . . . His strong hand tightened on the knife handle. Minter's neck was inches away.

Suddenly there was a crash from another room. Nick froze.

Minter raised his head with a jerk. "Drat that kitty," he said. "She's knocked over the fern again." He hurried out of the kitchen.

Nick stared at the knife in his hand, then at the spot where Minter had been standing. He dropped the knife and ran out of the apartment.

The pink-faced man was polishing a little brass lamp when Nick came into the shop. Nick's face was white; his eyes were like the eyes of a hunted animal.

Nick put the bag with the shell in it on the counter. "I'm returning the shell," he said in a shaky voice. "I want my money back."

The pink-faced man slowly opened the bag. Nick loosened his collar. The shop was as hot as it was the last time.

The pink-faced man looked up at Nick, surprised. "Your money back?" he said in his soft voice. "Is the shell no good? Is something wrong with it?"

"Yes . . . No!" said Nick, helplessly. He felt dizzy and confused.

The man's lips curved in an odd sort of smile. "I'm sorry, Mr. Weston, I don't give refunds."

Nick felt as if the heavy air of the shop were pressing in on him, choking him. "Take it!" he said, pushing the bag toward the pink-faced man. "Just take it!" His voice was a hoarse whisper. "I don't care about the money."

Nick dropped the bag on the counter and walked quickly out into the cold winter day.

The pink-faced man gently lifted the shell out of the bag and held it in his plump fingers. "You always come back, my friend," he said softly. He took a thin gold pen and a tiny label from the desk. Slowly and carefully, he wrote $150 on the label. Then he placed the label on the shell and put it back in the window. He looked up; a man was staring through the glass. Staring at the shell. The pink-faced man smiled.